Plains Cree

Blackfeet

Assiniboin

Yakima

WASHINGTON

Columbia

Cayuse

Nez Percé

Gros Ventre

MONTANA

NORTH

Misso

SOUTH

OREGON

Klamath

Flathead

Crow

Yellowstone River

Cheyenne

WYOMING

Por

Oglala

Niobr

NEB

Pawn

Modoc

Shoshoni

IDAHO

River

Snake

River

Great
Salt
Lake

Yosemite

NEVADA

Ute

UTAH

Arapaho

COLORADO

Smoky

KA

Mariposa

Paiute

Colorado River

Arkansas

PACIFIC

CAL

Mohave

Navaho

Zuñi

Hopi

ARIZONA

Comanche

Yuma

NEW MEXICO

FORNIA

Pima

Apache

Rio Grande

Mescalero

TEXA

OCEAN

M
E
X
I
C
O

Concho

FAMOUS AMERICAN INDIANS OF THE PLAINS

"Call out the roll of American Indians. Among them you may single out the most famous of all—the Indian of the Great Plains.

"His star rose like a meteorite over the wind-combed prairie. It flared briefly, and died." So begins S. Carl Hirsch's dramatic retelling of one of the most fascinating and often bitter chapters in the history of mankind. In the brief span of a hundred years every aspect of the lives of these Plains people changed completely. From poor, earth-grubbing tribes living in settled villages on the fringes of the Great Plains they became in a remarkably short time the wide-ranging, free-spirited "Buffalo Indians"—the ideal of the American Indian as pictured in everyone's mind. It was the coming of the horse that brought this change. As horses were lost, strayed, or stolen from the Spanish settlements to the south, the various tribes were able to tame them and to move out onto that great sea of grass which held a seemingly bottomless larder—the vast herds of buffalo. With their horses the Plains Indians could now follow the buffalo at will, and their lives became exciting and colorful. It was a life on horseback, and mounted, like the knights of old, they became a proud, warlike people— the chivalry of the Plains. This was their world, a world—as N. Scott Momaday, himself a full-blooded Kiowa, says in his foreword— "full of motion and meaning, worth looking into."

Continued on inside of back cover

FAMOUS
AMERICAN INDIANS
OF THE PLAINS

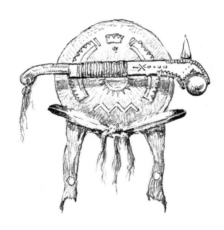

FAMOUS AMERICAN INDIANS
OF THE PLAINS

By S. CARL HIRSCH

Foreword by N. SCOTT MOMADAY
Line Drawings by LORENCE BJORKLUND

RAND McNALLY & COMPANY · CHICAGO · NEW YORK · SAN FRANCISCO

FRONT COVER: *The Last of the Buffalo*
by Albert Bierstadt
IN COLLECTION OF THE CORCORAN GALLERY
OF ART, WASHINGTON, D.C.

Book Design by
MARIO PAGLIAI

Library of Congress Cataloging in Publication Data

Hirsch, S. Carl.
    FAMOUS AMERICAN INDIANS OF THE PLAINS.

    SUMMARY: Discusses the history, culture, and legends
of the major Plains tribes and the effects of their contact with
the white man.
    1. Indians of North America—Great Plains—Juvenile lit-
erature. [1. Indians of North America—Great Plains] I. Bjorklund, Lorence F., illus. II. Title.
E78.G73H57 1973   970.4'8   73-7622
ISBN 0-528-82475-9
ISBN 0-528-82476-7 (lib. bdg.)

Copyright © 1973 by RAND McNALLY & COMPANY

Printed in the UNITED STATES OF AMERICA
by RAND McNALLY & COMPANY

First printing, 1973
Second printing, 1974

CONTENTS

C·M·Russell 1903

FOREWORD

A HUNDRED YEARS AGO the Great Plains were inhabited by a people whose culture was the last to evolve upon this continent—the Plains Indians. As their name implies, their style of life was determined in a real way by the landscape in which they lived their lives. They were people of the plains, plainsmen, as much at home there as were the tortoises, the magpies, and the buffalo. At one time there were perhaps fifty million buffalo on the Great Plains. And at the same time there were no houses, no roads, no fences. In every direction the earth reached away, unbroken, as far as the eye could see. There, as nowhere else, was the sun a deity, a constant and irresistible force, the source and essence of time and light and well-being.

The Plains Indian, in his relatively brief tenure as ruler of this vast landscape, became the archetype of the aboriginal American. In him was concentrated the color, the strength, the spirit of the open wilderness itself—above all the sense and expression of freedom.

For the Plains Indian was a nomad. To be confined was to him intolerable; to be enclosed—as he was eventually—unimaginable. His whole life was based upon the principle of mobility. His idea of the world —and of himself in it—was above all an idea of motion. He must move, and he must be free to move. He must come and go; and in his coming

11

and going he realized his destiny, his meaning as a man and as a race.

The culture of the Plains Indians is sometimes called the "horse culture," or the "centaur culture." The acquisition of the horse brought about a revolution among the peoples of the Plains, one of the great revolutions in human history. Before there were horses, the Plains Indians were in a sense imprisoned in their landscape. After there were horses, the world of these peoples was enlarged almost beyond belief. Hunters and warriors were known to undertake expeditions that required months —even years—to complete, over a range of thousands of miles. In Kiowa tradition there is a story concerning a party of hunters who traveled on horseback from the southern plains (in the vicinity of the Wichita Mountains in Oklahoma) to Central America (Honduras) and back.

The horse figures in innumerable examples of Plains Indian oral tradition, and not infrequently the horse is represented in heroic and even supernatural terms. Again with reference to Kiowa tradition, there is a story which has it that the tornado is the spirit of a wild horse that roams the sky. Another concerns a hunting horse whose owner, in a moment of cowardice, turned it away from battle; the hunting horse died of shame.

In the vignettes which follow, we have an epitome of the Plains Indians and their world. It is a world full of motion and meaning, worth looking into.

N. Scott Momaday

RIDERS OF THE DAWN

CALL OUT THE ROLL of American Indians. Among them you may single out the most famous of all—the Indian of the Great Plains.

His star rose like a meteorite over the wind-combed prairie. It flared briefly, and died.

His wild cry was once heard across a vast region where the silence was enormous. His fire was the one light in a dark wilderness that lay level around the full circle of the horizon.

Back in the early days of our nation, this tribesman rode in pursuit of huge buffalo herds. He was a freehearted wayfarer. His range was a double belt of short grass and tall grass prairie, extending from the edge of the Mississippi Valley to the foothills of the Rockies and from the Mexican desert to the Canadian tundra. He made for himself a style of living such as the world had never seen, full of daring and brilliance.

Where did he come from? Why is he gone? And what has happened to his horse-and-buffalo way of life?

Buried deep in the prairie soil are the bones of a small animal the Indians had never seen. This was *Eohippus,* "the dawn horse." Its kind had vanished long before the first human beings ever set foot on this continent.

Through the mists of time, all the horselike animals disappeared

OVERLEAF: *The Silk Robe*
by Charles M. Russell
COURTESY AMON CARTER MUSEUM, FORT WORTH

from this hemisphere. They wandered about the planet, the species evolving, gaining size and speed. Eventually, man in Europe and Asia tamed the horse to his needs. In the sixteenth century horses returned to the American continent, tethered on the pitching decks of Spanish ships.

The Spaniards who conquered Mexico held their prized mounts tightly reined, picketed, hobbled, and corralled. But in time, horses found their way into Indian hands. High-spirited, some animals ran to freedom across the wilderness to become the forebears of wild mustang herds.

In those early times, few Indians could find a livelihood out on the Great Plains. To a man on foot, chasing buffalo was an unpromising way to survive. Indian tribes fringed the open prairies. They hoed maize in the bottomlands, fished and hunted in the woodlands, lived a stationary existence in high-domed earthen lodges.

By 1750 a new kind of life style had spread northward across the Great Plains. Now the tribes were mounted and mobile. These were gal-

loping hunters, suddenly capable of living well on a single abundant game species, the buffalo.

Additional tribes secured horses and moved out onto the prairie. A dozen or more large tribes became year-round roving hunters, following the cycle of migrating buffalo, which numbered in the millions.

By the 1850s the end of this pattern of life was already in sight. But within that period of one hundred years, the Plains Indian fashioned an extraordinary culture. Each of the tribes remained distinct. But because they shared the common ecology of the Plains, they developed similar styles of living. They adapted themselves totally to the Plains environment. In turn, the natural setting remained wild and timeless, suffering little change at the hands of the wandering tribesmen.

Without the horse, the Indian was a hunger-haunted stalker of game, a grower of limited crops, a gleaner of wild roots and fruit. Once in the saddle, he became a wide-ranging huntsman, whose skill could keep himself and his family well provided. Within two or three generations, he achieved complete mastery of a new mode of living based on the horse and the buffalo.

He journeyed across one of the great natural hunting grounds of the world. His was not an easy or secure life. The climate was one of extremes—fierce suns of summer and the rage of high autumn winds led to slashing blizzards and deep cold. Hunting fortunes varied from feast to famine.

But even with simple weapons, the Plains Indian showed uncanny skill in bringing down big game. And as a horseman he was not surpassed either by the Mongol tribesmen of Eurasia or by the desert equestrians of Arabia.

The Indians of the Great Plains were men who believed in themselves. They flaunted their freedom. And they raced across the flatland for the sheer joy of it. Theirs was a society on the move. And its driving force was horse power.

HALF MAN, HALF HORSE

By FIRESIDES where Pawnee gather, they still tell of the Orphan Boy. Poor and lowly, he and his grandmother followed the wandering trail of their tribe.

In a spring season long ago, the head chief of the Pawnee learned of an unusual spotted buffalo calf, seen in the midst of a large herd. The chief pictured to himself the uncommon beauty of a spotted robe. And he offered the hand of his daughter in marriage to any hunter who would bring him the calf skin.

The Orphan Boy could only wonder at who would be the fortunate slayer of the buffalo calf. And then one day while the boy hunted rabbits, a strange and towering figure appeared. It was a dun-colored horse.

The boy clambered onto its back. Horse and rider sped like wild wind across the prairie. Far ahead was a vast buffalo herd. Suddenly the boy spied a bright flash of color among the brown beasts.

Quickly the young rider put an arrow to his bow. As his horse raced alongside the spotted calf, the arrow found its mark.

The Orphan Boy was to become a brave hero of the tribe. Astride his dun-colored horse, he rode to fame as hunter and warrior. And with his bride he lived in happiness. Or so it is told in the Pawnee legend.

The horse figures importantly in the old stories of the Pawnee, as it

18

does in the memories and dreams of every Plains tribe. For the horse carried the Indian to moments of triumph, abundance, and glory.

Throughout the eighteenth century there were no finer horses on the eastern Plains than those of the Pawnee. And few riders have ever outshone them in spectacular horsemanship.

Like most Plains Indians, the Pawnee mounted from the right side in Spanish style. Otherwise, there was little about these daring, agile horsemen that recalled the Spanish caballeros who had brought their steeds to America.

Carefully bred to the needs of life on the Plains, the Indian horse was also different from its Spanish ancestors. The typical Indian pony, a small but sturdy animal, was long-winded and durable. Unshod, he was a fast, surefooted hunting horse and a fearless charger in battle.

Tough as an oak knot, this animal withstood long periods of hunger and thirst. Winter and summer, he was a good forager, who could be counted on to find his own food when necessary. Intelligent and obedient, this mount took readily to special training for a variety of tasks.

The Pawnee war-horse learned to carry his rider into the very core of battle, leaping over the fallen, turning in tight circles under the slightest knee pressure, dancing constantly so as to make the most difficult target.

On the hunting range, horse raced buffalo neck and neck while his rider aimed the fatal shot. The pony knew how to swerve clear at the precise moment when the huge falling beast might lunge into his path, its sharp, curved horns still dangerous.

The training of both horse and rider was a lifelong process. From infancy the child sensed the rhythm of the horse. On the trail the mounted Pawnee mother carried the baby in the folds of her buffalo robe or laced into a cradleboard slung from her saddle.

Boys and girls rode bareback on their own ponies by the time they were four or five. Among their chores, youngsters were charged with the care of horses—keeping them fed, clean, picketed at night, exercised and rubbed down in the mornings. Boys spent most of their playtime riding and racing. Training constantly, they became skillful horsemen with a spectacular bag of tricks. They ran and leaped into the saddle, rode in every possible position, picked up objects from the ground at full speed.

A loose coil of rope around the horse's chest was an aid in trick rid-

ing. One feat was performed with the rider dropping down under the running horse and coming back up on the other side!

The young Pawnee became expert at guiding his mount with a touch, a word, a slight pressure of knee or heel. He learned to ride with both hands free to use the short bow, drawing arrows rapidly from the quiver on his back.

Pawnee riding gear was simple. Often the saddle was a thin pad, held by a rawhide cinch. A thong looped around the lower jaw of the horse served as the bridle.

The Pawnee became famous as a horse Indian. In the saddle, the tribesman was a graceful and dashing figure. He rode high and haughty, his vision extended, his range expanded toward every horizon.

Mount and rider appeared to be a single creature. Together they were like that mythical beast, the centaur, half man and half horse. As one they defied want and danger. On horseback the Indian was a match for the challenges of the prairie wilderness and for the power of his enemies.

In motion he was grace itself. His loose, fringed garments rippled in the wind, as did the flowing tail and mane of his steed. The mounted Pawnee warrior flaunted his decorations and trophies. And on proud occasions he even crowned his horse with eagle feathers or buffalo horns. His "painted pony" was often just that, daubed with the same flashing colors as his master. Many of the Indian ponies were natural pintos, bred not only for speed and stamina but also for a favorite combination of colorful markings.

Two centuries ago, untamed, free-running herds of mustangs thundered across the ranges. Once caught, wild horses could be broken and mounted only through the greatest patience and skill. The Pawnee had a way with the mustang. He excelled in horse talk—the grunting, cooing, whistling, clucking sounds that seemed to work on the animal like a charm. As trainer, he rubbed and petted until the range horse was no longer afraid of the human touch. Assured that he was in gentle hands, the skittish runaway would soon become a loyal companion.

However, capturing the wild mustang, or bronco, was not a dependable way of acquiring horses. Sometimes they were secured through trading. More often, horses were the fair prizes of battles and of raids.

In their keen desire for more and better horses, the tribesmen of the Plains changed their entire outlook on life.

Before Spanish horses found their way onto the western prairies, Indians had shunned any form of personal riches. White men might wrangle endlessly over gold, goods, land. Living simply, Indians were not interested in accumulating private property. However, by the eighteenth century, the Plains tribes did come to value the ownership of horses. In fact, horses were called "Indian money."

Mounts were owned individually and not by the tribe. Among the most respected men were those who were horse-rich. Trained hunting horses were the means for securing food. They were used in trading for goods, paying off debts. They were given in dowries. Horses were gifts that brought prestige and power to the givers. A good war pony was the means for gaining honors in battle. Many a Pawnee warrior picketed his prized mount outside his lodge and never went to bed without tying the rein to his wrist!

In hundreds of ways, the Plains Indian changed as he became horse-

21

OVERLEAF: *Smoke Signal*
by Frederic Remington
COURTESY AMON CARTER MUSEUM, FORT WORTH

borne. His pony was now part of himself, his hopes and dreams, and even his religion. His favorite horse would accompany him to the grave.

The entire lifetime activity of the tribesman centered around the mounted hunt and the horse raid. He cured his ponies of illness, trained them in obedience, and bred colts of excellent stock. Weapons and clothing, food and shelter reflected the needs of life in the saddle. The Plains Indian had become a mounted wanderer across the far reaches of a sun-filled, spacious land.

NOMADS OF THE PLAINS

"BREAK CAMP!"

At the earliest trace of dawn, the Cheyenne band was on its way. Quickly the tepee village disappeared. Down came the lodgepoles. Fires were quenched.

The cavalcade was forming, ready for the trail. Scouts were already out on diamond points, scanning the sweeping vistas of the prairie.

Camp leaders bawled out last commands. The men hurried their wives. The women shouted after the children. And the youngsters chased their yelping pups.

The scene was busy, noisy, frantic. And yet there was a kind of order to it all. From its waking moment to the last council fire at night, the roving band worked by plan. Hoofbeat and drumbeat marked the rhythm of Cheyenne life.

Every member of the group had an appointed part and place in the daily pattern of motion and change. Adults and children had their tasks to perform. Chiefs, scouts, warriors, horse grooms, tanners of hides, water carriers, buffalo huntsmen, cooks, weapon makers, elders—all had their duties.

In one such band, an old and toothless woman called Shiny Eyes carried a glowing coal in a buffalo horn from one campsite to the next.

25

OVERLEAF: *Indian Women Moving*
by Charles M. Russell
COURTESY AMON CARTER MUSEUM, FORT WORTH

Big Left Hand towered six feet three inches in his moccasins, and no hunting pony could carry his enormous weight. He became the chief arrow maker of the band.

Shot Foot, a disabled veteran of many battles, doctored the horses with care and skill, using secret salves and herbs. A widow named She-Bear was a specialist in treating snakebite.

The children had their duties. But there was time set aside too for games, social dances, and fireside tales.

The day's routine brought a noon stop and a quick lunch of pemmican, a prepared mixture of meat and wild cherries. Long before sunset, the day's march ended. There was still time before darkness to unpack, set up camp, water the horses, prepare the evening meal. Summer nights the band rested in the stillness of the starlit prairie.

The shifting Cheyenne band was a close-knit community. Hardship and personal sorrows were shared. And as long as some had food, no one starved. The poor and the sick, the elderly and the orphaned were cared for.

They had no jails. "A people that has no locks on its doors," the Cheyenne said, "can not tolerate a thief." Crime was rare, and theft almost unknown.

In case of a dispute, a council meeting was called to act as court. The decision was usually fair and just, and all parties to the case generally obeyed the ruling. Public opinion throughout the group was strong, and few defied it.

The roving life gave rise to a breed of leaders who led by common consent. Every tribe had a number of chiefs and headmen. No single man could ever speak for the entire tribe. The Plains Indians frowned on a leader who grasped for personal power. Like everyone else, the chief performed his share of tribal duties, hunted for his own food, and received no pay for his leadership. A chief was a respected tribesman, whose advice was sought in making tribal decisions. On the trail the band chief's duties included planning the movement, selecting campsites, leading the hunt.

The Cheyenne had societies and clubs to which every member of the tribe belonged. There were special societies for women and for young people of different ages. Some performed functions in ceremonies, in battle, and in the hunt.

The military societies patrolled the camp at all times, keeping order. One of their most important responsibilities was to guard against any individual who might venture out alone on a buffalo hunt and thereby scare off the herd. The culprit was endangering the food supply of everyone. And the punishment for such an act was harsh.

No society was allowed to attain too much power. The various military groups took turns at camp police duties, serving for limited periods of time.

Most of the music making and dancing was sponsored by the societies. Some were secret rituals. But the entire tribe joined in the main ceremonies, which often had a deeply religious meaning. Many dances were linked to hunting and war. Others commemorated peace, victory, the passing of adults and young people into new stages of their lives.

Dazzling costumes and trappings were the pride of every society. They vied with each other in the splendor of their garb.

Fantastic masks, face and body paint turned the dancers into exotic creatures. They wore ornate, plumed headpieces. The bustle, or "crow," a sunburst of multicolored feathers, glittered as they danced.

The dancers were bedecked with beaded sashes and armbands, painted robes, and radiant roach bonnets. They waved decorated lances and feathered banners aloft. They shook rattles made of gourds and turtle shells.

Some dances were simple. But others sent the tribesmen leaping and writhing, building speed and frenzy to a spinning, blazing, reeling climax.

For the Plains Indian the drum was the heartthrob of the world. And the dance set him into rhythm with the mystic powers that controlled all of life and nature.

The prairie Indian was the originator of a wide array of equipment that was uniquely suited to his nomadic existence. The Plains tepee was his invention. This portable lodge was a sturdy, year-round dwelling. It consisted of long poles lashed together to make a framework for a covering of animal skins.

An opening at the top served as a chimney. And in order to improve its ventilation, the Plains tepee was designed as a lopsided cone, with the back portion more steeply sloped than the front. From the peak downward toward the doorway was a long, narrow smoke slit. The opening could be adjusted for good draft and for changing wind direction by means of a set of movable flaps. In warm weather, the tepee covering was rolled up partway.

The lodge was readily set up and dismantled. Some tribes used a basic framework of four poles. The Cheyenne pitched a tent on three poles, rounding it out with a dozen more.

In a remarkable way the abode of the Plains Indian was quickly transformed into a carrier of freight, the travois. In preparing for travel, the tepee lodgepoles were fastened to the saddles, their ends dragging on the ground. The tepee skins were then folded and fastened across the trailing poles. On this platform could be piled a great quantity of baggage. Often children or old folks rode the horse travois.

Weapons underwent a marked change as the Plains Indian became a horseman. The bow was shortened for mounted use and given more curvature. Lance and club, ax and knife varied according to the needs of a people in almost constant motion. Among these hard-riding people every article of daily use assumed a distinct appearance. These were the special artifacts of the Plains Indians—and no other.

Across a vast region the Cheyenne roamed free. They stalked the grazing buffalo herds, which in turn followed the seasons.

In late summer signal fires on the prairie brought the wandering Cheyenne bands together. The full tribe met at an appointed place for a period of feasting and ceremonials. This was also a time for courting among the young, for horse-trading, and for feeling the strength and unity of the tribe. A great tribal hunt was organized, which brought in a large store of meat to be dried and smoked for the months ahead.

Autumn windstorms soon turned the dry grassland into a billowing yellow sea. Geese headed southward in the valley flyways. The Cheyenne bands gathered plant foods and prepared winter quarters.

Icy winds howled down from the highlands. The scattered bands of tribesmen found places where water was available and forage for horses plentiful. Fuel was gathered. The roving Cheyenne were now halted for a worrisome season. Blizzards and bitter cold gripped the Plains area. Gradually supplies of meat, beans, roots, berries, nuts, honey dwindled.

By early spring the horses were lean and light-headed from hunger. Ice still sealed the streams. Thunderheads massed in the skies. But it was time to break winter camp. The hunters were restless and eager for the sight of the buffalo herd.

These were the most difficult months for travel. Storms delayed the journey toward the hunting ground. Often the band had to ford swollen and icy streams. But at last came word that the buffalo had been sighted.

Now it was a matter of speed. The entire company strained with a common effort. Ahead was food, as well as the many other things which the buffalo supplied. It was all up to the horses now.

This was the Cheyenne nomad life. At times it was indeed harsh, onerous, risky. And yet this was the chosen livelihood of a people who thrived on the western prairies.

The Cheyenne were not tied to any plot of ground, rooted to any landhold. No tribe was more wide-ranging across the central plains. At the beginning of the nineteenth century, Cheyenne camps spread over an area from the Black Hills on the high western rim of South Dakota to the broad flowage of the lower Missouri River.

Moving widely and constantly, the Cheyenne made contact with many other tribes. With some, the Cheyenne maintained friendly relations. By tradition, however, there were sharp animosities among many of the Plains tribes and with those in the surrounding hills and forests. Cheyenne fought Crow. And Blackfeet clashed with Sioux. An era of increased tension and bloodshed was soon to begin.

In the year 1803 came an event which was to change life on the Great Plains. Unknown to the Indian tribes who had made it their home, the Plains region changed hands in a bargain between white men called the Louisiana Purchase. For three cents an acre, the United States bought the entire region from the French, who had acquired it from Spain, who had in turn won it from France.

To the Indians the Plains were common ground. Most of them had never been aware that the Plains belonged to anyone. Many had never even laid eyes on a white man.

AN EYE FOR AN EYE

IN THE DEAD OF NIGHT, a Blackfoot raiding party crept toward an enemy village.

The Shoshoni of the Red Deer River had returned only recently from the white trading post. And the raiders fully expected to seize a rich stock of weapons and supplies.

The Blackfeet pounced upon the Shoshoni lodges with knives drawn. But there was no resistance—only the strange stillness of death. Smallpox had wiped out every member of the village.

The Blackfeet, unwary as yet of white men's diseases, helped themselves to everything they could carry off. It was only a short time until smallpox broke out in the Blackfoot camp. Wild with fear, the tribesmen pleaded with their medicine men for help. But the contagion spread. More than half the tribe died. The rest swore vengeance on the white men, the bearers of plagues.

The Blackfoot Indian asked the sun for recovery from sickness. In facing the doorway of his lodge toward the east, he bid the sun awaken him each day with the gift of life and health.

The great ceremonial occasion of the Blackfeet was the yearly Sun Dance. This festival was opened by the Sacred Woman, wearing a towering headdress of ermine fur and eagle feathers. The woman chosen to lead the Sun Dance was one favored by the sun-god for her purity of mind and body.

Almost all of the Plains tribes performed the Sun Dance. But just as no tribe "spoke Indian" or worshiped in the same manner, so also there were no two tribal observances of this ritual that were exactly alike.

The Sun Dance was usually held in the late spring or summer months. It was elaborately prepared, centering upon a tall pole around which was constructed the open frame of a large lodge. Here the tribe gathered for a number of days of devout worship. A rhythmic dance circled sunwise around an altar.

For many tribes this was a time for thanksgiving and prayer for health and bounty. Some stressed the theme of self-sacrifice. Others made this mainly the occasion for young men to make their vows of service to the tribe. The tribesmen cleansed themselves at sweat baths. They fasted for days.

The Blackfeet came to the Sun Dance in their best garments, riding their finest horses. They wore special bone necklaces and weasel-skin ornaments, which had religious meaning.

Painted Blackfoot warriors danced one at a time in the center of the arena. Some pierced the skin of their chests with skewers. Thongs from the central pole were bound to the skewers. The dancers rose on their toes, straining and tearing against the thongs in order to inflict pain on themselves. In a trance induced by hunger and pain, the warriors sought visions that would give them divine guidance.

For the Blackfeet, the Sun Dance was the most sacred of all their holy days. The occasion grew more solemn each year as the tribe became increasingly warlike and life on the Plains grew more dangerous.

Through the entire first half of the nineteenth century, the Blackfeet were to become known as the most hostile of all Plains tribes. By reputation, they were fierce and cruel, the sworn foes of white men who crossed their paths.

Their hatred was born of fear. These tribesmen seemed to sense that the white intruders threatened their way of life and their very existence. Some dark vision foretold the doom of their people.

• • •

On July 27, 1806, moccasined Blackfoot scouts silently trailed a party of white men. These were members of the Lewis and Clark expedition, returning from the west coast on their exploration of the vast

33

OVERLEAF: *When Sioux and Blackfeet Meet*
by Charles M. Russell
REPRODUCED BY PERMISSION OF AND COPYRIGHT
BY BROWN & BIGELOW, ST. PAUL, MINNESOTA

new territory which had been acquired by the United States in the Louisiana Purchase.

The Blackfeet approached the white men smiling. Early the next morning they made a brash attempt to grab weapons and horses. In the scuffle, two Indians were killed. The tribe never forgot this first encounter with the new United States government.

The 1800s brought a rapid change to the Great Plains. The United States, a young and vigorous nation, was expanding swiftly. From the American seaboard the West appeared as a mysterious wilderness, full of challenge and hidden opportunity. White men were pressing westward, driving Indian tribes before them across the Mississippi and into the prairies.

The buffalo plains became a field of battle. Rivalries among Indian tribes turned more fierce than ever. Westering white men soon encountered the mounted tribesmen of the Plains, hostile and vengeful. Comanche and Kiowa, Sioux and Blackfeet—the mere names rang terror in the hearts of white men.

Blackfeet found themselves in the direct path of America's westward migration. Trappers and traders surged across the trails of what is now Montana and toward the passes that breach the Rockies. Wagon trains creaked westward through Blackfoot territory in the northern plains. Soon to come were the miner and missionary, sodbuster and trooper, rancher and railroader.

The Blackfeet became the scourge of enemy Indians and migrant whites alike. To their prowess as buffalo hunters, the Blackfeet added the skills of war. Masters of stealthy ambush and lightning raid, they struck with fury. The blood-chilling war whoop echoed across the vast Blackfoot country.

Disciplined and well trained as fighting men, the Blackfeet moved on hand signals from their leaders. They attacked by surprise and vanished into the wooded hills to regroup for a new assault.

The warriors of this powerful tribe were tall and strongly built. Some wore their hair loose, with one narrow forelock hanging down in front and cut square at eye level. On bodies burned dark by wind and sun, they painted bright red and yellow designs. Before a battle they cut skin wounds into their arms and legs. They sought in this way to fortify themselves against pain, to heighten their own anger against the enemy, and to draw the pity of the gods.

Scalping was common on the Plains. This practice had long been fostered by white men in their attempts to use Indians against Indians for their own purposes. White men not only indulged in scalp-taking but also offered cash bounties for the scalps of Indian men, and of women and children—it didn't matter. However, scalping was less popular on the Plains than "counting coup" as a method of collecting war honors.

Coup is a French word meaning "a blow." A coup was a daring act of touching an enemy in battle with a stick, a weapon, or with the bare hand. For each coup, the warrior was privileged to decorate himself with an eagle feather, a wolf tail, or some other tribal symbol. The Blackfoot badge of battle honor was a patch of white weasel skin sewn to the shirt.

Each tribe had a defined method of reckoning the value of various kinds of coups. The warrior who took the greatest personal risks received the highest honors. The first coup was always a dangerous one. A warrior might rush forward to touch a "dead" enemy—only to have him spring to life suddenly with knife in hand.

The Blackfeet defied the rifles of the early white frontiersmen. From a safe distance, they drew the fire of these single-shot weapons and then moved in for the kill. In order to be fired again the old muzzle-loaders

had to be filled with powder, a ball rammed home with a long rod, the pan primed, and the flintlock adjusted. Meanwhile an Indian could charge 300 yards, getting off twenty deadly arrows as he came. Later, when breechloaders and repeating rifles were introduced, the Blackfeet were able to barter horses for these types of firearms.

The Blackfeet were among the last of the Plains tribes to acquire horses, which passed tribe-to-tribe from Spanish sources in the south. The horse did not spread through the Blackfoot country until the middle of the eighteenth century. To the Blackfeet, this strange animal seemed "large as an elk and tame as a dog." Their name for the horse was *ponoka-mita*, meaning "elk-dog." Once mounted, the Blackfeet quickly became able horsemen. In battle they would win the respect of their mounted foes, including the United States Cavalry.

The Blackfeet spread southward, invading the territories of their neighbors in bold, slashing attacks. They became a horse-rich tribe, proud of their mobility and power. To capture a foe's best horses by cleverness and cunning had a double value. The raid strengthened the raiders and weakened the enemy in the same stroke!

Plains life turned more and more violent. Tribe against tribe, Indian versus white man, the clashes spread. Revenge was the war cry, north and south. War on the Plains reached a climax of terror and agony.

The torture of captured enemies became a cruel type of defense. In one way or another, news of the savage treatment of prisoners got back to the enemy camp. It was an intended warning to any who dared to attack.

As the toll of raids and captures, tortures and killings mounted higher, all kept count. The contest of vengeance, an eye for an eye, brought ghastly acts of savagery. Neither side showed any mercy.

To the Indian boy growing up on the Plains, life appeared to be a ceaseless struggle. From earliest childhood, he was caught up in the game of war. His ambition was to live as a warrior and to die a hero.

GROWING UP BRAVE

LITTLE BIRD AWAITED his chance. The Arapaho boy had long looked toward the moment when it would be his turn to break in one of the wild young broncos.

In the middle of the stream stood the dappled pony, snorting, twitching nervously. After hours of shouting and chasing, a dozen boys had succeeded in getting the untamed animal into the water chest-high.

Now came the crucial moment. Little Bird made a dive and swam underwater to the horse's side. Suddenly the boy lunged, flinging his arms around the horse's neck. "Hang on!" his friends screamed.

The pony reared high, threshing the water to wild foam. Repeatedly the animal bucked and leaped, fuming and splashing.

Little Bird held on, his arms and legs coiled tightly around the rampaging bronco. Deftly the boy threw a rawhide rein around the horse's head. The pony pitched a mad fit again and again, plunging, writhing, floundering. And still the Indian boy stayed glued in place. At length the animal quieted down, exhausted, its chest heaving. Little Bird spit out a mouthful of water and grinned.

The boy gently stroked the quivering, fretful colt. He whispered soothing words into the animal's ear. Slowly he guided the weary bronco out of the water onto the riverbank. Little Bird slapped his mount on the rump. Horse and rider galloped off across the prairie.

For Little Bird and the other boys of his band and his tribe, bronco-breaking was part of growing up. From their youngest days, Indian children on the Plains learned the arts of survival. They were taught to ride and shoot, to hunt and fight.

With his first bow and a quiverful of blunt arrows, the boy shot game birds and small animals. A favorite sport with his friends was rapid shooting, keeping as many arrows as possible in the air at one time. The Arapaho boy developed skill in marksmanship, shooting at bundles of grass. More often, he aimed at a moving target, like a rolling hoop or a buffalo chip tossed in the air. In time, he was allowed to go on his first buffalo hunt.

The Indian boy learned attack from the hawk, concealment from the toad, courage from the cornered coyote. On a flat terrain with few obvious landmarks, he trained his eyes and his mind to map the slightest of signs. Play was training. Popular sports were archery and wrestling, horsemanship and stalking. The youngster was instructed in the secrets of the hunt and the trail.

As a rule the teachers were the older folk. The storytellers were not merely entertainers. They also taught the young boys and girls how to make weapons, build shelters, sew and decorate clothing, preserve and cook food, deal with danger.

The veteran warriors were also the historians of the tribe. They told of their own growing-up days. And in their storytelling, the elders stressed the ideals of bravery and valor. The Arapaho boys learned the stories by heart. The tales of the warpath were undoubtedly the most popular of all.

By the time he was fifteen, Little Bird was ready for the ritual of young manhood. He found for himself a lonely cliffside, where he perched like a hawk for four days and nights. During this period he fasted and prayed for a vision that would guide him into his adult life.

The Indian of the Great Plains deeply believed that the spirits communicated with him by means of visions. In his mind's eye, figures appeared to tell him how to live and how to die. They transferred to him some of their supernatural gifts. Only the tribesman who sought and received such visions might serve his people successfully and deserve their honor. Such dreamlike images would guide him for his entire lifetime.

Little Bird had prepared himself for his vision quest, purifying his body with sweat baths and clearing his mind for a revelation. Weakened

by hunger and dazed by the heat of the sun, he stood waiting, silent and motionless as the rocks about him.

At last he seemed to see the figure of a fierce bird which befriended him and gave him some of its power. The young man uttered a solemn pledge that he would use that power to serve and safeguard his people. He made the Arapaho sign, the right forefinger, pointed skyward, alongside the nose. "I ask the sun to hear my vow!" Little Bird cried out.

He now sought out his grandfather, an aged hero of the tribe. From the old man the boy secured a bundle of secret charms and sacred relics that were to bring him special protection against evil and danger. The bundle included a pipe and a set of face paints, a leather medallion, and a hawk's wing.

Little Bird was now sure that he was ready to take his place as a full-fledged adult. But his parents thought otherwise. They advised him to wait until he was older.

The young man grew restless shooting rabbits, tending the horse herd, and helping the hunters and warriors prepare for their duties. He felt he was ready to join a war party.

Horse raiding was part of the routine of Arapaho life. A raiding

41

OVERLEAF: *The Captive Charger*
by Charles Wimar
THE ST. LOUIS ART MUSEUM

party might be formed by a group of ambitious young men eager to gain honors and to win the favor of the young women of the tribe. A quick attack was planned on an enemy camp. The plan stressed surprise and daring. Intended neither for killing enemies nor for taking scalps, the objective of the raid was simply to capture horses.

In the dark of one autumn night, a small party left the Arapaho camp on its way to a horse raid against the Pawnee. At a considerable distance, a lone horseman followed unseen.

At dawn, the warriors stopped to rest. Suddenly Little Bird appeared on his pony, uninvited. The men were angry. It was the war party leader, Lone Bull, who decided to allow the boy to remain as part of the raiding effort.

Two more days of swift travel took the party into Pawnee territory. Their style of movement now changed. The Arapaho spread out, alert for telling signs and wary of spies.

Was the stalker being stalked, the watcher being watched? Every raider noted the sounds and shadows. He was careful not to scare into flight any birds that might alert the enemy. Each man found his way stealthily through gullies and draws, staying off the hillcrests.

They were now stripped down to breechclouts and had packed away every eye-catching item. Lone Bull took off the three red-dyed feathers, the symbols of his coups in battle. Horse raiding was a deadly game. And one man was personally responsible for the safety and success of the mission. In such a war party as this, the leader's word was law.

Lone Bull called his men together by the arranged signal of the screech-owl call. He had found traces of the enemy's previous camp!

Little Bird now saw the skills of these warriors come into play. Keen eyed, they put together dozens of clues. They could clearly see the size of the enemy band from the number of lodges which had been pitched. From hoofprints they reckoned the size of the enemy's horse herd. In what direction did the Pawnee band go? How old was the trail? Bits of displaced rock, crumpled brush, nibbled grass led the raiders on their way. By nightfall, they were scouting the enemy from a nearby hillock.

In the darkness the raiders performed a silent and solemn ritual. They dared not even light the ceremonial pipe but passed it symbolically among themselves. Plans were carefully reviewed in whispers. Little Bird was instructed to remain in hiding with the horses.

From a wooded hillside, Little Bird could see the men in the half-light, moving toward the sleeping Pawnee village. Suddenly, shots rang out. The raiders had fallen into a trap!

As Little Bird watched anxiously, the Arapaho took shelter behind a large rock. Both sides exchanged fire, and the battle raged.

To the Arapaho their position appeared hopeless. They were pinned down behind the rock, unable to escape. Suddenly they heard the clatter of hoofbeats coming toward them. Little Bird was speeding to their rescue, bringing the riding horses with him!

The Arapaho mounted up swiftly and rode hard, not looking back. They knew the Pawnee would be in hot pursuit. The ponies of the war party sped headlong across the plain. Galloping hooves pounded the dry earth. Was the enemy gaining on them? This was a race for life!

At a signal from Lone Bull, the raiders exploded in all directions, leaving their pursuers dazed and confused. The raid plan had foreseen the likelihood of a chase. Each member of the Arapaho party had a separate and devious route for the return.

In a canyon deep in their own territory the Arapaho warriors reassembled. The raid had gained them no horses. But the members of the war party had escaped with their lives, thanks to the courage of a boy.

It was sunset when the Arapaho neared home, and the autumn prairie foliage was ablaze with fire colors. In the distance their camp was full of tumult. The raiders were being eagerly greeted by their fellow tribesmen, who waved banners, shouted words of praise, and sounded drums, whistles, rattles.

To the amazement of the welcoming party, it was not Lone Bull who rode in front. The place of honor was given to Little Bird! The other warriors rode zigzag patterns behind him.

The rescue of comrades under fire ranked high in the scale of Arapaho battle honors. A dance was held in honor of Little Bird. His mother and sisters prepared a celebration feast. In a ceremony that night, the young man was recognized for his fearlessness.

This was the occasion on which he assumed a new name. Little Bird was no more. The young Arapaho would now be known the rest of his life as Grey Hawk.

This was the way a young tribesman was welcomed into adult status. His people acknowledged that he had undertaken the duties of manhood and mastered the arts of survival. Everyday life was a test of raw courage on the buffalo plains.

THE MOONS OF WINTER

ASSINIBOIN REMEMBERED a year "when winter came twice."

Long before the Frost Moon (November), the prairie was a vast, glazed sheet. Out of a sky black with rage, sudden and violent storms roared down from the northland.

Stunned and surprised, the tribe took cover quickly. Then, after a mild spell, the season again turned raw, snowy, and bleak. By now the tribe was well settled along several miles of the Poplar River in what is now northeastern Montana.

Winter was a season of rest and healing for both people and horses. This was a time of no buffalo hunts and no war parties. And yet there was plenty to do.

In the lodges the women were busy on the last of the cold-weather clothing. The children and the old people had begun spending a lot of time together. The men were at work on the first of many winter projects—repairing riding gear, creating the colorful trappings of the raid and the hunt, making new weapons.

The Assiniboin bow began as a length of oak or ash, carefully chosen for toughness and springiness, cut and formed to the proper shape. Layer after layer of wet buffalo sinew was carefully applied, coated with animal glue and powdered white clay. The last operations added colored and patterned decorations. Often the bow makers inlaid pieces of buffalo horn.

Drawn by a well-muscled wrist and arm, the Assiniboin bow was a powerful weapon. On the hunt, the tribesman often embedded his arrow so deeply into the buffalo's back that it protruded from the animal's underside. In combat, the strong bow gave speed and distance and accuracy to the arrow's flight.

A bundle of arrow stock hung high in the winter lodge, being cured by the smoke of the fire. From this bundle, a few shafts were chosen from time to time. They were smoothed and straightened and trimmed to a fixed length, from the warrior's chest to the tips of his outstretched fingers.

The Assiniboin used six kinds of arrows, differing in points and feathering. Half-feathers were glued in place to give the arrow the proper action in flight. The arrow maker kept buffalo sinews in his mouth as he worked. Wet rawhide shrinks as it dries. And the Indian maker of weapons used this principle in order to bond the parts securely together.

Some arrows were knob headed or dull pointed for use in target shooting or in hunting small game. On a war party or on the buffalo trail, the tribesman carried a full quiver of thirty arrows. These had sharp points made of flint or bone. Iron arrowheads were fashioned from the strap metal of barrel hoops, which the tribesmen secured at trading posts.

Longtime traders with the French and the English, the Assiniboin had early use of many of the white man's trade goods. This was among the first of the Plains tribes to acquire guns and steel knives, mirrors and glass beads, wheat flour and coffee. However, in later years the tribe came to shun all of the white man's products and influences.

Fiercely independent, the Assiniboin tribesman returned to a traditional style of life as it had developed out of his tribal past. His forefathers had needed nothing from the white man—and neither did he!

The history and lore and legends of the Assiniboin were not in books. They were in the minds of their people, deeply remembered since childhood days. The winter lodge was a special kind of school. Here the teachings were passed person-to-person from one generation to the next.

One evening at the fireside a father turned to his children and made a circle sign with his fingers. Did they know what it meant? The circle, he explained, was the symbol for the sun. So began a period of instruction in the use of sign language.

Speaking with hand signs was an art highly developed by the wandering Indians of the Great Plains. This was the common mode of communication between tribes, each of which had its own spoken language. Sign language was carried on by swift, graceful movements. In simple gestures, one tribesman might tell a member of another tribe where he had come across a water hole, sighted a wolf pack, or seen a prairie fire set off by lightning. Sign language was important training for Indian boys and girls.

In snowtime the Assiniboin child gathered in the shared wisdom of his people. His very survival would depend on how carefully he listened. But this was more than just practical instruction. He learned who he was out of the proud record of the past. He became absorbed in tribal stories of heroes and their sacrifices, hardships endured, battles won, the goodness of the gods, and the meaning of ancient myths.

On a bitter cold day, a mother gathered all the children of the band to share a treat she had cooked. She told them the tale of the old woman who was out alone on the prairie one night finishing up her work of butchering and drying buffalo meat.

Suddenly the old woman was surrounded by enemy warriors, who threatened to take her captive. But first they all sat down to eat their fill.

As they drowsed by the fire, the old woman snatched up a firebrand and ran off into the darkness. When they realized she was escaping, the enemy warriors gave chase, following the torch. The Assiniboin woman, knowing well the terrain, ran toward a cliff's edge, threw the lighted stick out over the precipice, and hid in the brush. The enemies followed the firebrand. Unwittingly, they plunged over the high crag to their deaths.

While blizzards raged outdoors the children listened to such fascinating stories told by people they loved. The old legends were a delight to hear. They also taught the important values of life and the ways of kindness, reverence for all living things, and the common rules of courtesy.

In the presence of white men Indians often appeared solemn, sullen, unsmiling. But within the family circle, there was much fun and laughter. The adults taught with the use of humor. "Always speak softly," a father would instruct his youngsters, "unless you notice that the

lodge is on fire!"

By means of a jest, the people of a band often corrected improper behavior. This was an effective way to deal with a troublemaker, a gossip, a cruel parent, a boaster.

Late one afternoon a young man called Red Dog came limping into camp, bleeding from many wounds. After his sister bandaged him, he came to the council lodge to tell what had happened to him.

Red Dog was not well liked by the tribe. He shirked his duties, talked much about his grand intentions, but never joined a war party or performed well in the hunt. Nevertheless, the council gathered to hear his story.

Early in the day he had ventured out on the prairie to hunt birds, Red Dog said. At some distance from camp, he encountered three Blackfoot scouts. Drawing his knife, he defended himself against these enemies.

Red Dog described the battle, acting out every detail. He thrashed about violently in the council lodge, almost falling into the fire. Making fierce knife thrusts through the air, he showed how he inflicted

49

OVERLEAF: *Mystery of the Buffalo Gun*
by Frederic Remington
THE HOGG BROTHERS COLLECTION,
THE MUSEUM OF FINE ARTS, HOUSTON

damaging wounds while receiving a few cuts himself. In the end, said Red Dog, he had routed the foe single-handed.

The headmen of the council listened carefully as they shared a pipe. At length Chief Black Bear passed the pipe to Red Dog. The pipe had sacred meaning, and few would dare to tell lies in its presence.

"If your story is straight, young man," said the aged chief, "then you will not object to smoking the straight-stemmed pipe."

Red Dog backed away. "I have told you the truth," he shouted. "There is no need to prove it!"

Black Bear leaned forward. "You were observed from a distance by Bright Cloud. She says you were apparently asleep while riding. And when your horse stumbled, you were thrown, falling into a ravine full of briers."

Red Dog jumped up and fled from the lodge. The chief smiled and then chuckled. Soon the entire tepee rang with laughter from everyone. The boaster became the laughingstock of the camp.

The old chief was well respected. Black Bear was a member of a cult of warriors who drew some sense of power from a bear seen in a dream. He wore a bear-claw necklace. And his knife handle was made out of a bear's jawbone, from which protruded sharp teeth. His eagle feather headdress was flat topped, in the manner of most northern tribes.

At his call, the families of the band filed into the large council tepee, which was made with twenty hides. For an important gathering the crier of the band was authorized to take an item of value from every lodge, to be returned when each family arrived for the meeting.

This tribe set aside time for ceremonies to honor the young. A winter birthday was an especially joyous occasion. Dancing and feasting marked a young girl's first achievement in handicrafts. Boys were given recognition for hunting skills.

The January Moon of Hard Times brought aching cold. In the frosty nights, the tribesmen sometimes heard a loud explosion. It was a cottonwood, burst open by the freezing of its sap.

The Assiniboin were skilled in winter living. Their lore was rich in the experiences of years long past when the tribe had lived far to the north. They were the only Plains tribesmen who "turned their backs on the North wind," facing the doorways of their lodges to the south.

They built especially sturdy tepees. Around them were constructed high snow fences made of woven brush. The families added to their lodges an inner liner of hide, which kept out the wind and cold. This liner came up about shoulder-high all around the interior and was attached with thongs to the lodgepoles.

These tribesmen were strong believers in hospitality. The warmest place in every tepee was covered with robes and reserved for visitors.

Assiniboin were famous for their cooking. Dried buffalo meat was tough to chew. But this tribe knew how to make it tender by long boiling.

Their pot was a bag that hung from a tripod over the tepee hearth. Smoking-hot stones were drawn from the fire and dropped one by one into the water to bring it to a boil. From that style of food preparation came the Assiniboin tribal name. It means, "They who cook with the use of stones."

In the Assiniboin calendar, the month of March was called the Sore Eye Moon. Snow blindness was a common ailment in this season for those who went out on the white prairie in search of small game or fire fuel. But even in the coldest weather, the children dressed warmly and played outdoors. On a piece of hide they skidded swiftly down an icy slope. Or else they built tepees out of snow.

During that season came the time for the selection of a new band chief. The old chief had served long and well. But he was ready to step aside for a younger man.

There was little doubt how the people would choose. One man had proved his worth beyond all question. Three Horse had made his mark in combat. He was a hunter of rare skill. Most of all, he was known and loved for his kindness to children and for the warm welcome to be found in his lodge by everyone. On the hunt he killed game not only for himself but for the poor as well.

Assiniboin men took pride in the length of their hair. Three Horse had hair that almost reached the ground. His weathered face made him look older than his twenty years. He was an expert with the lance and an owner of fine dogs.

For weeks the headmen and elders had been preparing the ceremony for the selection of the new chief. The women were just finishing a splendid headdress fit for a hero. It featured a pair of buffalo horns, with a trailing double row of eagle feathers.

Only one question remained. Would Three Horse accept the awesome responsibility?

On a morning clear and cold, the entire band assembled. Three Horse was offered the sacred pipe by the elders. A great cheer rang out when he took it soberly from their hands.

Now the long solemn ritual began—prayers of hope, vows of service, chants and dances, gifts and feasting. In the council lodge, the people sang out their joy and faith in a new leader.

It was now the Frog's Moon (April). But the river ice was still hard, no buds had appeared, and the prairie was white and cold.

An old legend of the Assiniboin pictured the summer season as water contained in a bag. The bag, according to the ancient tale, was carried southward each autumn by flying cranes. In the spring the cranes always returned, bringing the bag with them.

But in this strange year, the warm weather came late. The storytellers knowingly explained that the cranes had tarried along the way.

The food, kept deep frozen in underground caches, was almost gone. A snowshoe party was sent out for fresh meat. Luckily, they were able to chase down a few buffalo and catch them floundering in a snowdrift.

Then at last came the first joyous days of spring. That year it was the young chief himself who led the Buffalo Dance. Three Horse paid homage to the herds. Pipe in hand, he humbly appealed to the spirit of the buffalo. On behalf of his people, he pleaded for permission to harvest enough game for their needs.

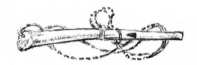

WHERE THE BUFFALO ROAM

"TSI'RUP" MEANS "BUFFALO" in the Crow language. And in Crow life on the western prairie the buffalo meant everything.

The Crow Indians knew all there was to know about this amazing animal, inside and out. The Plains buffalo was a huge, whiskered, hump-backed, heavy-headed beast, weighing a ton or more full grown. Its innards were oxlike, with a four-chambered stomach and an extensive set of ribs. The male looked like two halves of different animals grafted together, with massive foreparts and a lightweight rump.

The American buffalo, or bison, were native to this continent. Although powerful, these beasts were easily panicked. For protection, they moved in vast herds, needing nothing but grass and water.

In addition to buffalo, the prairie supported a variety of grass eaters. Among them were herds of pronghorns, colonies of prairie dogs, large numbers of rabbits, rodents, and seasonal wildfowl. These in turn were the prey of wolves, bears, pumas, snakes, predatory birds.

In any natural setting, prey and predators, plant and meat eaters, the hunters and the hunted exist in a state of delicate balance with each other. As long as no destructive forces upset this equilibrium, life continues to be supportive and stable.

Neither Indians nor buffalo remained in one place long enough to do the environment any serious damage. At the high point of their remarkable culture, around the year 1800, there were no more than 200,000 Plains Indians. The buffalo outnumbered the Indian 300 to one. On the open prairie, this shaggy beast had no significant natural enemies other than man. And as long as the human inhabitant of the Plains used the buffalo simply for his own needs, the species was never threatened.

Because they followed the yearly cycle of the herds, the Plains Indians developed a unique style of life—fluid and fast-moving, venturesome and colorful. And thus the buffalo set the pattern for man's ways.

Buffalo hide was the multiuse leather, canvas, cloth of the Plains Indian. It was adapted to a thousand uses by the women of each tribe.

The Crow women used a variety of methods for preparing hides. Rawhide was made with the skin staked to the ground or stretched in a frame. With a scraping tool the Crow women cut away bits of meat and gristle, also trimming the skin to the desired thickness.

The making of pliable buckskin was a more complicated process. A tanning acid was applied. After it was sun-dried, the skin was softened by vigorously working over it with various instruments. The final step usually was curing the leather by smoke treatment.

The Crow women were highly skilled in skinning animals, staking out, stretching, and dressing the hides. In addition to buffalo skins, they used those of elk, antelope, and deer. They had a feeling for the natural qualities of these materials.

The Crow garments took their shape from the skins from which they were made. Simplest of all was the one-piece woman's dress, fashioned from a single whole skin with an opening for the head to slip through. Most of the year the men wore short buckskin shirts, or tunics. The footwear for everyone was moccasins. Men's leggings consisted of two long tubes, fastened at the waist. The breechclout completed the male outfit, hanging like a short apron, front and back.

The women sewed with the awl in one hand and the bone needle in the other, drawing the tough sinew through the hide. To their simple costumes, the Crow Indians added a wide array of decorations. They used such natural materials as porcupine quills, nut shells, quail feathers, hawk claws, ermine tails. In later years they acquired glass beads made in Italy, and they embroidered artistic ornaments such as the world had never seen.

These dwellers of the grasslands had a keen sense of beauty. They created a wide variety of arts, including painting, music, and dance. Paints and dyes were made from earth pigments and vegetable juices. They decorated their lodges and equipment, their weapons and tools. And they adorned themselves as well.

They did not copy from patterns. The design took form under the deft fingers of its creator. Each was a one-of-a-kind original work of art, expressing both the culture of a people and the personal mood of the artist.

The tribesman took care and extreme pride in his work, putting his own individual artistry into a flute, a painted buffalo skull, or a long-stemmed pipe. Whether he was making a small whistle out of a turkey bone, decorating a shield with sacred symbols, or fashioning a fire-making drill, the Crow Indian was a craftsman.

The Crows traveled light and easy. Their pursuit of the migratory buffalo left no time to build durable structures. They stayed nowhere long enough to plant and harvest a crop.

They carried no textile looms or pottery kilns. Little time was spent in weaving baskets, in carving wood or stone. Instead they developed crafts of many other kinds, using parts of the buffalo—hide, horns, bones, sinews.

Mainly the buffalo was a food supply. The Plains Indian was resourceful in his methods of obtaining, butchering, and preserving meat.

In the years before he had the horse, the Indian tried a variety of difficult hunting methods. Buffalo herds were stampeded over cliffs and driven into enclosures. Tribes used "the surround," a method of encircling the animals, sometimes setting grass fires in order to entrap them. It was only on horseback, however, that the Indian found the buffalo a food source both plentiful and reliable.

Each spring, small groups of these animals came out of sheltered, scattered winter homes in the river valleys and wooded hills. Like merging mountain streams, the herds swelled in numbers as they moved together toward the open plains. By the thousands they followed the new grass northward, flowing along at amazing speeds, considering their bulk. The earth trembled under their mass. It took three days for a summer herd to swim across the Missouri River!

The Plains Indians found little joy in killing the "humpbacks," as they called them affectionately. It was hard, necessary work. And the hunt was organized as efficiently as possible. The tribesmen worked as

OVERLEAF: *The Buffalo Hunt*
by Charles Wimar
WASHINGTON UNIVERSITY GALLERY OF ART, ST. LOUIS

a cooperative team, wary of the hazards of the hunt and experienced in the ways of the buffalo. The only keen sense that this animal possesses is that of smell, and the Indians stayed downwind until they were ready for the chase.

From a distance, the joint assault on the buffalo herd was carefully organized in order to get the largest and the best kill. To the extent that the hunters moved at a signal by a prearranged plan, this was a group effort. But each hunter pursued his own quarry, facing his dangerous task alone. It was a single mounted man against an enraged and charging brute ten times his size!

Hazards lay hidden in the brush—a concealed rock, perhaps, or a badger burrow. A horse's misstep meant more than just a bad fall. The downed hunter fell directly into the path of stampeding hooves and deadly horns.

Now came the moment for the warrior to test his courage and the fine edge of his pony's training. Stripped down to breechclouts and weapons, the bowman lashed his horse into the pursuit.

Knowingly he chose his prey and raced the thundering beast stride-for-stride. Straining hard, the warrior gained speed. The horse was now galloping free and unreined. The arrow was in place. Suddenly the plunging target was a bow's length away.

Coolly taking aim just below the buffalo's hump, the bowman drove his arrow deep under the ribs, toward the heart. A twang of the bow-string and a clean kill. That was the mark of the master hunter!

A good day's teamwork for the hunting band might bring in food to last for a month or even a season. The women were soon at work butchering the kill, loading the pack horses with great slabs of meat.

Roasted or boiled, fresh buffalo meat was just right to the Indian's taste. The Crow were famed as sausage makers. Much of the summer's kill provided dried and smoked meat for the lean months of winter.

Buffalo skin, tough and waterproof, served hundreds of purposes. In the making of clothing these hides were used with the hair side either in or out, depending on the season. The skins provided bedding and robes. Parts of the hide were especially useful in making cold-weather garments: caps, mittens, and hard-soled moccasins.

Buffalo cowskins, a dozen or more sewn together, made a sturdy covering for the Crow tepee. When the Crow faced a stream crossing, their simple solution was to build tublike bullboats. These were made by stretching buffalo hides over frames of boughs.

Sinews served not only as sewing thread but also as bowstrings. From the horns of the buffalo, the Indians made cups and spoons. Tools such as awls and needles were fashioned from polished bone. Soft skin or organs of the animals were stretched over wooden hoops and used as buckets.

A variety of toys were derived from the buffalo. Balls were made of sewn-skin covers stuffed with hair. In winter, Crow children played in the snow on sleds with buffalo ribs as runners.

Crow warriors used circular shields made from the tough, thick chest hide of the bull as protection against arrows. Bow handles were strengthened with sections of buffalo horn.

Riding gear of all kinds was crafted from buffalo parts. A sore-footed horse was fitted with rawhide horseshoes. Ropes for halters, reins, hobbles, lariats were made of rawhide and of braided buffalo hair. Rawhide saddles were stuffed with hair padding.

The Indians made glue out of buffalo hooves. From parts of the animal they boiled up tallow for candles, acids for tanning, oils for lubricating and softening. With firewood scarce on the Plains, the Indians generally used dried buffalo dung as fuel for their fires.

At ceremonials Crow Indians gave thanks for the bounty of the buffalo. They danced to the beat of a drum covered with buffalo rawhide. And on the altar they placed a painted buffalo skull.

The Indian of the Plains stood in sharp contrast to the white man who migrated there. Nothing revealed the distinction more clearly than their unlike attitudes toward the buffalo. For one, the buffalo was a livelihood. To the other, the species was hardly worth keeping alive.

There the differences began. But in every phase of their lives, white men and red men were on opposite sides of a great divide. Between them stood a barrier which few ever crossed.

TWO WAYS OF LIFE

FROM HER QUIET HOME in Virginia, little Cynthia Ann Parker moved with her family to the wild Texas frontier. In the year 1836, her life once again took a sharp turn in a wholly new direction. Nine-year-old Cynthia Ann was kidnapped by Comanche.

That year, clashes on the southern plains between Indians and white men reached new levels of violence. Massacres and atrocities were charged against both sides. Kidnapping was not unusual.

Some white men had never quite given up their old idea of making slaves of the Indians. In the slave markets of the Carolinas, Indians in shackles were still being put on the auction block. Indian children were stolen from the Plains tribes to become the captive servants of white ranchers in Texas and Mexico.

In turn, tribesmen raided the white settlements, killing and destroying. Sometimes they took captives.

In such a raid Cynthia Ann Parker was seized by a Comanche band that ranged across the area of northern Texas known as the Staked Plains. The little white girl was adopted by the tribe. She grew up as an Indian woman, part of a roving band.

When she was eighteen, Cynthia Ann became the bride of a rising young war chief, Peta Nocona. Of their children, one of them, Quanah, was destined to be a famous Plains Indian leader.

Apart from her origins and her pale skin color, Cynthia Ann became a Comanche in every way. She was one of the few who ever crossed the line dividing two separate worlds.

Although they shared the same environment, the contrast between the white frontiersman and the Indian plainsman was striking. They lived by totally unlike codes, differing in their daily needs, their values, and their goals.

To the white man the acquiring of property and possessions was important. The Indian had little interest in belongings and none in the personal ownership of land. To one, the region was a "wasteland" until he had built on it, fenced it, tamed it, stocked it with plants and animals to suit his tastes. The other dreamed that the Great Plains would remain forever as a wild range for free-running game and hunting tribesmen.

The Indian wanted life simple and the prairie unchanged. The newcomer risked danger to try his luck in a wild country, fired by hope and driven by the blazing goal of success. You might hear it in the language of the "Go West!" promoters. A man could "strike it rich," "reap a harvest," "make a killing," "win a bonanza." The farseeing among them imagined the grasslands flourishing with products for the eager markets of the world, teeming with trade and industry.

The Plains Indians were part of the natural pattern. They worshiped the sun, called themselves by animal names, lived on wild foods, attuned their lives to the cycle of the seasons. The settlers saw themselves in a life-and-death war with nature.

One was a nomad; the other attached himself to "grass roots." One lived by hunting and gathering; the other by raising livestock and growing crops, running mines and mills, living off "the fat of the land," and "doing a land-office business."

To the white man, the Indian was a "savage" who had no churches, schools, books, written laws, or central government. To the Indian, the white man was a marauder and a land thief in spite of all his claims to being educated, pious, and civilized.

On the southern plains, white missionaries appeared frequently to try to convert the Comanche to their beliefs. Chief Peta Nocona told them: "We will wait and see how well your religion stops white men from cheating Indians."

His wife, Cynthia Ann Parker, had more than one opportunity to return to her former way of life. Instead she remained among the tribesmen, adopting their customs and dress, their language and religion.

The life of the women of the Plains tribes was arduous and wearisome. They carried heavy burdens. On their shoulders fell almost the entire task of maintaining the family and the household under the difficult conditions of constant movement.

The Plains way of life divided men and women into sharply differing roles. Hunting and fighting were the business of the men. And women took care of everything else. Should a man be seen raising a lodgepole or drying meat, there was usually talk about him in the tribe. "Since when has so-and-so become a woman?" the men would ask each other.

If Cynthia Ann Parker objected to carrying out the burdensome routine of Comanche wife, she never complained. Perhaps she found some fulfillment in the splendid handicrafts in which the women of the tribe excelled. Certainly she took pride in watching her son grow up.

Young Quanah became an expert horseman, a sure shot with the bow and arrow. Like the other Plains tribes, the Comanche were being hard pressed by white newcomers, whose frontier of settlements was gradually moving across the Indian hunting grounds. Quanah joined in the swift raids on white outposts and in mounted clashes with those fierce cavalry troops, the Texas Rangers.

On a blustery autumn day in the year 1860, the Comanche band was camped on the Pease River, an alkaline stream wandering through the northern Texas plateau. With no warning, the Rangers fell upon the Indian camp, their six-shooters blazing. Chief Peta Nocona was among the scores of tribesmen who fell dead. As young Quanah hid in the brush, the Rangers sped away. One of them was carrying off Cynthia Ann Parker.

In that single day, Quanah lost both his father and mother. The fifteen-year-old boy, filled with sorrow and hatred, took a vow of revenge against the whites. He became a daredevil raider, striking at ranches and trading posts, swooping down on wagon trains and mining camps. Quanah was the terror of the Santa Fe Trail, carrying on forays along the southern pioneer pathway across the west.

By the time he was twenty-two, Quanah was made a chief of the Kwahadi band. Among Indian tribes, men did not rise to chiefdom merely because they were the sons of chiefs. A warrior became a leader only because of his own achievements. And he remained chief only as

long as he could retain leadership through the respect and confidence of his people.

Quanah was not a man who sent others into battle. He was in the forefront of every raid. Under fire, his personal courage and example inspired his tribesmen to fight on.

No Plains tribe was more zealous in safeguarding individual freedom than were the Comanche. They kept the power of their tribal government and their leaders to a minimum. But in Quanah the Comanche had a chief whom they fully trusted. His fierce style was never to surrender. Even when his warriors were hopelessly overwhelmed and surrounded, Quanah's uncanny skill in battle led to escape.

On the attack, his Kwahadi struck hard, whirled and fled. Quanah and his "red raiders" were notorious across the southern plains. The army offered a bounty for Comanche scalps and a rich prize for the fearsome Quanah, dead or alive.

The chief was a big man, lithe and muscular. His face was a coppery mask, thin-lipped and sober. He wore his hair in long queues, and his garments trailed braided fringe. A single shell earring and a lone

OVERLEAF: *Intercepted Wagon Train*
by Charles M. Russell
COURTESY AMON CARTER MUSEUM, FORT WORTH

eagle feather were his decorations. On his mount, Quanah's poised bearing expressed dignity and defiance.

The Comanche were among the greatest of the Plains horsemen. Under Quanah's leadership, the Kwahadi band claimed a herd of 15,000 horses. As the buffalo dwindled, these horses were traded and sold for food and supplies.

Texas Rangers and United States Cavalry struck again and again at the Kwahadi in a deliberate effort to destroy their stock of horses. Their strategy was to control the springs and water holes. Across that parched land, many of the Comanche ponies died for lack of water.

By the 1870s, Quanah and his people were making their last stand. The buffalo, once abundant, were rarely to be seen. Soldiers and hide hunters were slaughtering the last of the wild game.

On June 27, 1874, Quanah led an attack to drive out the white buffalo hunters who had taken over the trading post called Adobe Walls. However, sheer courage and determination were not enough against the heavily armed and fortified outpost.

By the third day of the battle, Quanah had led one assault after another. The steady fire kept pouring from the stockade. The Comanche chief who had promised never to retreat knew he couldn't win. His horse had been killed. Blood oozed from a wound in his shoulder. His strength was gone. This was Quanah's final struggle to save his people.

That year the Comanche bands, one after the other, surrendered to the military. The following spring Quanah was still at large. He would hold out until he was ready.

One June morning a dignified group of Indians walked into Fort Sill. This was Quanah and the members of his council. The man who had never surrendered, never signed a treaty, never bowed to the white man was giving up at last.

68

THE FALL OF THE HUNTER

FROM WHITE MEN the Kiowa Indians learned two new ideas. One was the notion of "prison," the other the concept of the "reservation." In Kiowa language, the word was the same for both.

In 1868 the United States government had a reservation prepared for the Kiowa. It was a narrow strip of land between the Washita and the Red rivers in what was known as the Indian Territory, later the state of Oklahoma. In the center of the Kiowa district, the army had built a military stronghold, Fort Sill.

Once they entered the reservation, the Kiowa knew their free-ranging days were over. They could not leave without a pass. Life, they believed, would become tedious, wearisome. They would have little voice and few choices in running their affairs. A tribe which had been hunting game for generations would be forced into poor, small-scale farming or living on government rations. A people free as eagles were being told to take up chicken raising and grubbing in the soil.

"The Kiowas are not ready for barns, churches, houses, farms—not as long as one buffalo roams the plains!"

The tribe's spokesman was Satanta. If Indian warriors often appeared hideous and frightening in their war paint, their intention was

OVERLEAF: *Ceremony of the Scalps*
by Frederic Remington
PHOTO COURTESY REMINGTON ART MUSEUM,
OGDENSBURG, NEW YORK

exactly that—all the better to strike fear into the hearts of their foes. Large-boned and squint-eyed, Satanta painted his face for striking effect. His hair was thick, jet black, and hung down to his immense shoulders.

He was a fearsome figure. And yet under that mask of ferocity was a strange sense of humor. Perhaps Satanta laughed in the way that men sometimes do when they are facing hopeless odds.

Among the Plains tribes there were warriors who were called "contraries." They sometimes rode their horses seated backward, spoke in riddles, performed personal acts of heroism in battle that few reasonable men would attempt.

Satanta often acted in such a mocking, clowning, prankish way. Somewhere he had acquired an army bugle and learned how to play it. In several skirmishes, he confused the cavalrymen by blowing the bugle call for retreat at a time when the troopers were supposed to advance!

He mimicked the military by wearing a blue officer's jacket, complete with brass buttons and gold braid. When the army commanders summoned Satanta to a "peace" parley, the Kiowa leader sometimes sent word that he was too busy hunting. Or else he might arrive late and sit through the meeting whittling on a coup stick.

In a quiet but forceful way Satanta was eloquent. The Kiowa leader was a rare combination of fighter and statesman. Very often a tribal chief who had distinguished himself on the battlefield was no match for the whites at the treaty table. But Satanta proved to be a tough bargainer, who was well able to express the problems and needs of his troubled people.   .   .   .

And yet every tribe of the Plains felt that the days of their freedom were numbered. The strangest part of this entire tragic story is that white America seemed totally unable to understand the attitudes and feelings of the Indians. Most Americans earnestly believed that their government was being kind, and even generous.

The white man had no notion why the Indian should cling so stubbornly to his religion, his language, his customs. Nor did it make any sense to him that the Indian was dissatisfied to live within the confines of a farmstead. Because farming was the occupation of most white Americans, they saw no reason why the Plains Indian should not be eager to turn himself into a "typical American farmer."

The Kiowa could feel the white man's corral closing about them.

They were being rounded up and driven into a fenced-off tract which was only a tiny corner of their former hunting range. The chief goad was hunger.

Kiowa scouts peered over the rimrock of the Cimarron and scanned the broad valleys of the Arkansas. There were no large buffalo droves to be seen. But from a long way off they could hear the deep bark of the big-caliber rifles. Whites were busy slaughtering off the last remaining animals.

By 1871 the migrating buffalo of this continent had been divided into two distinct herds. The divider was the North Platte River, well-traveled pathway across the Plains, the route of the Union Pacific Railroad and of the wagon and stagecoach and mule trains headed westward.

In the north the buffalo were still able to find some refuge in the hills and wooded valleys. The southern herd was an easy target for an army of expert hide hunters.

Most of them carried the new Sharps 50-caliber rifle, a heavy, long-range weapon, too expensive for Indians to own. It was deadly accurate up to half a mile. At that distance the buffalo did not see the flash of the gun and hardly noticed its sound.

The sharpshooter spotted his prey, settled himself behind a clump of sagebrush, spread out his ammunition, and went to work. Picking off the grazing animals one by one, he never stampeded the herd.

He was not the archer on horseback in need of food for his people. This was the market hunter, in the cold-blooded business of selling hides.

As the riflemen moved to new sites, the skinners came along with their wagons. They took only the hides. The southern prairies were strewn with stinking piles of rotting flesh, carrion for buzzards and coyotes. Never in history had such a butchery of wild animals taken place anywhere. Hundreds of thousands of buffalo skins were sold in St. Louis for a dollar apiece. The hide men had a few profitable years. United States officials and army generals boasted openly that once the buffalo were gone, the Plains Indians were in their power.

The Kiowa and other tribes struck back at every new attempt to take their hunting land, their livelihood. They resisted those schemes that would make them poverty-stricken dependents of white men, who could control their lives by withholding their rations. And they fought against every effort to abolish the tribal form of government, the only means still left to the Plains Indian for dealing with the authorities in Washington.

Certain forms of popular government had existed for ages among the Indians. But although they represented a democratic government, white officials ruthlessly undermined the informal self-rule within the tribes. When it suited their purposes, the United States agents insisted on dealing with a chief as though he were an all-powerful tyrant. At the same time, they tried to "soften up" the leaders with bribery and personal gifts, or else with threats.

On occasion the whites played off one tribal leader against another. At times they even tried to replace a troublesome chief with one of their own choice.

In Satanta, the United States authorities had a frustrating, baffling problem. The Kiowan eluded their every scheme and made them appear ridiculous. He taunted them with his jests, outwitted them in battle. Many times they thought they had the chief cornered, only to have him slip away.

In the spring of 1871, a message was sent to the Kiowa asking them to sit down at a peace conference with General of the Army William T. Sherman. When Satanta appeared, he was arrested and imprisoned. The army could hardly have devised a more terrifying punishment for this wayward rebel.

74

Satanta was a restless, untamed man who typified the spirit of his liberty-loving people. To this hunter of the Plains there was nothing more threatening than to be "penned into a narrow space, shut off from the winds and the sun."

But while Satanta was in jail, his people did not rest. Now the Kiowa raids took on their full fury. The tribe plundered and pillaged the countryside. Their assaults were like wildfire and equally damaging.

From Washington came word to release Satanta in order to halt the attacks. Once again the roguish Satanta had the laugh on his captors, who sheepishly turned him loose.

But it was not long before Satanta was jailed again. In his narrow, dark cell in Huntsville, Texas, the Kiowa chief paced like a caged bear. The confinement at last broke his buoyant spirit. Something snapped in his mind. The jest was over. Satanta lay on the floor of his cell for hours, staring blankly at the sky through the tiny barred window.

One day the guards found him in a pool of blood, his wrists slashed. As they carried the huge form of Satanta down a second-floor corridor in a litter, the Kiowa chief suddenly sprang to his feet. He crashed through a window and plunged to his death in the courtyard below.

Ever since the Kiowa first appeared on the Great Plains, elders of the tribe had kept a calendar that pictured on calfskin hides the events in the life of their people. In the hard winter of 1875–6, the calendar told how the tribe was forced by the army to turn in their weapons, trade their horses for cattle and sheep. Dismounted and disarmed, the Kiowa were a helpless people.

Not only were the buffalo disappearing. The Indian pony was rapidly becoming extinct. The Kiowa tribal calendar reported 1879 as the "year of the Horse-Eating Sun Dance." The buffalo were so scarce that the starving tribesmen were forced to butcher their remaining ponies.

In "winning the West," United States government leaders dealt harshly with "hostile" Indians. At times they dealt even more ruthlessly with "friendly" tribes.

HOMELANDS AND HOMESTEADS

ON A CHALK BLUFF high over the Niobrara River, a caravan of heavily laden ox wagons groaned to a halt one day in the hot summer of 1867. Civil War veterans and their families had come to claim land under the Homestead Act.

As the men pounded in the stakes for property lines, they were being watched in silence by Indians. This was the homeland of the Ponca. It had been granted to them in a signed treaty. The small tribe had given up claims to all other territory; in return, the Indians were guaranteed permanent rights to the strip along the Niobrara.

If they would only turn themselves into peaceful farmers, the Ponca had been told, the government would give them every assistance. Above all, their land would be secure forever.

The Ponca had taken the United States government at its word. Now they were learning that treaties with the Indians were made only to be broken.

The Homestead Act offered a settler 160 acres on western land. He had only to stay for five years and pay the fourteen-dollar filing fee in order to make the land his own.

A million men were discharged from the army following the Civil War. Many trekked westward. Emigrants from abroad were streaming

76

into the United States. Thousands of people headed for the tall grass prairies to try their luck at homesteading.

The settler came with soaring hopes. Building himself a house from blocks of prairie sod, he hitched a hog-nosed plow to his ox team and cut a fresh furrow into the loamy earth. He was wary of troubles like drought, grasshoppers, and Indians. And to him, the Indians were just that—one more nuisance to deal with.

Surveyors eyed a straight line of sights and dragged their measuring chains across the open prairie. Rectangular pieces of the Great Plains were being shaped into states. And in the golden autumn of 1867, Nebraska came to statehood.

In this vast, flat country the state makers used few natural boundaries. They drew their border lines on the compass points. And they paid no attention at all to the traditional territories of Indian nations.

The Ponca, a docile and defeated people, could see their homeland vanishing. This was an uprooted tribe. Repeatedly, their people had been driven from places where they had sunk roots, established villages, and buried their dead. They were buffeted by the larger tribes. And now they found themselves at the mercy of the white newcomers. To resist meant war. And the Ponca were too weak and powerless to maintain a standing army and to devote their manpower and their energy to costly military supplies.

In the winter of 1869, the Ponca were sending appeals to Washington to honor the two treaties in which the government agreed "to protect the Poncas in the possession of the tract of land reserved for their future homes, and their persons and property thereon, during good behavior on their part."

In the Congress of the United States, a strange event was happening at that moment. On February 16, 1869, the Senate ratified a treaty with the Sioux Indians granting them the same land which had been deeded to the Ponca!

Were the white men who talked about "civilizing" them really out to destroy them as a tribe, the Ponca wondered. Were they now to be thrown into a war for their own homes with the powerful Sioux? In the end, neither tribe would have the land.

United States Army commanders had learned a lesson from those few occasions when Plains tribes had managed to stand together—and had won the day! Now a wide range of schemes were being used to keep

OVERLEAF: *Indian Warfare*
by Frederic Remington
THOMAS GILCREASE INSTITUTE OF
AMERICAN HISTORY AND ART, TULSA

the tribes divided and at odds with each other. If possible, the whites tried to split tribes into warring factions.

One army plan was to enlist Indians as soldiers and scouts. The Ponca were offered this option. Were the tribesmen facing starvation? They could sign up in the service, be assured of three meals a day and army pay.

The Ponca refused. In many of the battles then raging on the Plains, Indians were being sent to fight against Indians. As reported in American newspapers, it was "good Indians against bad ones." Members of some tribes had been forced into what Indians saw as a betrayal of their own people. The cavalry's "Pawnee scouts" were especially hated by the other Plains Indians.

In Washington the government spent little time pondering the problems of the "friendly" Ponca. New settlers wanted the Indians' land. Someone was sent to tell the tribe that their treaty with the United States, their deed to land along the Niobrara, was a worthless piece of paper.

The bringer of this news was an Indian agent, a type of official appointed by the government to deal with the Indians of a certain tribe or region. These agents were hand picked by officials in Washington. But they were not chosen for their sympathy or understanding of Indian needs.

The agents achieved great power. Many were hopelessly corrupt. Money, food, supplies promised to the Indians by the government passed through their hands. They connived with merchants, who supplied shoddy goods to the Indians, the food often spoiled and inedible. Bribed by sodbusters and ranchers, railroad and mining companies, the agents ousted the Indians from their native lands.

Soberly the Ponca filled the pews of a small church on a raw winter morning in January 1877. In the pulpit was Edward C. Kemble, representing the United States government. His message was brief and curt.

"The Great Father at Washington says you are to move!"

The site chosen for the Ponca was a far-off land they had never known. The government's plan was to consign many of the Plains tribes to tracts within the so-called Indian Territory. This region was already crowded with tribes that had been cleared out of the eastern half of the continent.

Many tribes had been pressed into these reservations through a long series of broken agreements. Each treaty drew tighter boundaries around them. With their hunting grounds taken from them, the Indians were reduced to begging food from the government. Once proud, these tribesmen were stripped of all faith in themselves, reduced to poverty that put them at the mercy of the cheating merchant and the land-grabber, the military commander and the civilian Indian agent.

The Ponca hardly protested. But their feelings were expressed by a chief who said: "We have given up land that sustained our people for a thousand generations. In return we receive rations that hardly last a day."

Unable to resist, the Ponca began the long march southward. It proved to be a disastrous journey. Sickness took a savage toll of the Ponca. For two months the tribesmen marched 500 miles under the prodding of troopers. Suffering hardships of many kinds, they endured tornadoes and floods. At journey's end, the Ponca were straggling lines of wretched people, their dull eyes empty of hope. They buried their dead along the way. Formerly a tribe of more than 700 members, their numbers were reduced to almost half that many.

The Indian Territory was far worse than they had feared. As they passed through the reservations of other tribes, the Ponca saw little but hunger, sickness, and privation. Some of these exiled Indians had tried "dust farming" in this drought-ridden area and made an effort to raise scrawny cattle on small plots of sun-scorched land. They were ill prepared for such a life.

Accustomed to the high arid plains, the Ponca suffered from serious illness in the hot lowlands of Oklahoma. Malaria and other strange fevers ravaged the tribe.

"We are like cattle," said Chief Standing Bear, "who have been driven into a corral on our way to a sure death."

The chief had lost a married daughter on the long forced march. When his sixteen-year-old son died, Standing Bear loaded the body into a cart. He and thirty of the tribesmen set off for their old homeland on the Niobrara. The chief had pledged to the dying boy that he would not be buried in an alien land.

Starting out in a blizzard, the party headed north. They would have starved except for the help of friendly tribes along the way, who shared with them whatever little food they had.

The army was quickly alerted to the fact that the group had "escaped." A telegram from the War Department reported: "Thirty Ponca

Indians have left the Indian Territory without permission. Return these Poncas to the agency where they belong." The government was not going to let the runaways set an example for other tribes on reservations.

When Standing Bear and his followers arrived on the Niobrara, the army was waiting for them. The tragic plight of the Ponca came to the attention of a few outraged whites. An Omaha newspaperman, T. H. Tibbles, brought their case to public attention. Tibbles went to the churches of Omaha for public support of the Ponca.

To the surprise of the government, the Ponca appealed their case in court. Chief Standing Bear appeared before United States District Judge Elmer S. Dundy to plead in behalf of his people.

In the packed courtroom, Standing Bear was a brilliant display of color in his chief's regalia, complete with necklace of bear claws and beaded buckskin garments.

The chief opened his speech by raising his right arm high for all to see. "That hand is not the color of yours," he told the court, "but if I pierce it, I shall feel pain—just as you would. The blood that might flow is the same color as yours. I am a man. The same God made us both."

Before the Ponca leader was finished, the courtroom was in tears. Standing Bear made a strong argument for the right of an Indian to appeal his case in an American court. In his decision, Judge Dundy admitted that he was deeply moved by the Ponca chief's words.

"An Indian is a person," was the judge's ruling, and therefore his legal rights had to be respected. Judge Dundy also declared that he "could not legally force the Poncas back to the Indian Territory to remain and die in that country against their will."

The Ponca had won a victory. The ruling was hailed as "historic." And yet it restored neither to the Ponca nor to any other tribe the homelands of their forefathers.

The Ponca remained a divided tribe, the two halves separated by 500 miles. The homelands they once knew were changing forever. Soon there were frontier boom towns, cattle herds grazing on the buffalo grass, files of telegraph poles tall against every horizon, and endless miles of barbed-wire fence.

The prairie was dotted with mining camps and farmsteads, army forts and land offices. Wagon ruts grooved the plain, and the wilderness was overlaid by a web of rails.

SUNSET ON THE PRAIRIE

THE OMINOUS SOUND of thunder echoed one spring morning of 1867 in the North Platte country. A party of Sioux scouts stared skyward in amazement. There was not a storm cloud to be seen!

In the ancient Sioux belief, thunder was the voice of the gods. However, what the scouts heard that morning was an ungodly blast touched off by men. From a steep butte, the Sioux caught sight of the thunder makers, a construction crew blasting rock with gunpowder to lay a bed for a railroad.

No one had asked the Indians for approval to lay tracks across their land. In sober councils that spring, the tribes pondered the meaning of this new invasion. Few leaders realized fully how serious was this threat.

A pair of slender rails would obviously bring a new trickle of white men into the Indian country. What the tribesmen did not know was that the railroad was an ever-widening funnel which would pour into the West an entire new civilization. The Spanish horse had changed the Indian way of life. The "iron horse" would change it even more!

At a fireside gathering of chiefs, a Sioux leader arose to pour out his anger and bitterness:

"Hear ye, my brothers! The white chiefs have laid down their rails before asking our yes or no. They are now pretending to deal with us for land they have already taken by conquest. Are we to be treated as children? Their presence here is an insult to the spirit of our ancestors. Are we to give up their sacred graves to be plowed for corn? Brothers, I am for war!"

This was Red Cloud, powerful leader of the Oglala Sioux. He was an awesome fighter, a battle-marked warrior with eighty coups to his credit. Red Cloud was named for a fiery meteorite that inflamed the skies of the Sioux country on the night he was born. He was respected by his people, while whites regarded him as a foe to be feared.

Tension mounted as the Union Pacific railhead moved steadily westward 500 miles—from Omaha to Grand Island and from North Platte to Cheyenne. The prairie resounded with steel mauls hammering rail spikes. Drums of Cheyenne and Arapaho and Sioux tribes beat out the war dance. Ever louder grew the hoofbeats of the United States Cavalry as the federal government began a huge buildup of troops.

Soon the trains began to rumble and hoot and smoke their way across the Great Plains. And now Indian fury turned to raging violence. Construction crews were ambushed. Trains were attacked.

At Plum Creek, Indian warriors had hitched their horses to a culvert and had torn it loose. They had watched as a freight train jumped the embankment and scattered its cargo over the landscape. In great glee, the warriors had tied the ends of the colorful yard goods to the tails of their ponies and had raced across the plains, trailing plumes of ribbon, calico, and satin.

Red Cloud's Sioux raiders attacked the railroad again and again. The Indian leader knew that the white man's steel band could no longer be ripped from the prairie. And yet he kept trying to force the intruders to pay some attention to Indian demands and Indian needs.

In an effort to soothe the outraged Sioux, United States government officials invited a group of tribal leaders to Washington. In early June 1870, Red Cloud and other chieftains found themselves at the top of the dome of the Capitol viewing the city. The two-week visit was designed to dazzle these dwellers of the prairie with the wealth and power of the United States government. Accordingly, they were taken to all the tourist sights. The military gave them an impressive display. The 15-inch guns of the coastal batteries were fired for them. In the roar and flash they watched the shells scream five miles down the Potomac.

Finally, the Indian leaders were taken to the White House to meet President Ulysses S. Grant as well as other government leaders. Red Cloud was respectful but not overawed. He told the president that it was the whites, not the Indians, who were bringing bloodshed and human suffering to the Plains.

"Our nation is melting away," the dignified Indian leader said, "like the snow on the hillsides where the sun is warm."

In the next days the chiefs were informed by government officials that they and their tribes were expected to move to the reservations, give up their Indian ways, and settle down to a life of dirt farming. When the Indian leaders protested, the whites brought out signed treaties which they said included all these provisions.

Red Cloud angrily charged the white officials with deceit. He cried out that the treaties had not been properly read to the chiefs when they signed them. He had traveled a long way to prevent more spilling of blood, the Sioux leader declared, but peace could not be achieved through lies and fraud.

"Do the whites want peace?" he stormed. "It is very simple. Let them keep their feet from the Indian trails. Let them not disturb the buffaloes and the ponies grazing in the valleys, nor the Indian children sleeping in the sun."

That night one of the Sioux chiefs tried to commit suicide in his hotel room. Saved from death, he wept bitterly as he explained that he could not return to face his tribesmen with the truth about what was in store for them.

Red Cloud was ready to go home. But against his will his hosts put him on the train to New York City, where he was to appear before a large public meeting at Cooper Institute. The Sioux leader knew he was facing a hostile audience that had been given a distorted view of American Indians. But with simple eloquence he stirred the hearts of his listeners.

"You have heard of us only as murderers and thieves, but we are not so," he said. "We have children just as you do. We want to live in peace just as you do. We do not want riches, only what is right and just."

By the 1870s most of the Plains Indians had been moved into reservations. The remaining tribes found themselves invaded, embattled, surrounded. The army had unleashed total war. In the battles of Sand

OVERLEAF: *Her Heart Is on the Ground*
by Charles M. Russell
THOMAS GILCREASE INSTITUTE OF
AMERICAN HISTORY AND ART, TULSA

Creek and the Washita, troops had assaulted whole Indian camps, attacking the male and female inhabitants from the youngest to the oldest.

A chain of forts jutted across the prairie skyline. Each year more railroads spanned the Great Plains and fanned out in all directions. Every train brought ranchers and farmers, promoters and town builders.

In 1874, gold was discovered in the Black Hills. By treaty, this region had been pledged to the Sioux forever. It was their sacred land. Generations of Sioux had worshiped here amid volcanic peaks that seemed to speak with the voices of ancient deities.

The United States government in that December of 1874 suddenly ordered the Sioux out of the Black Hills. The tribes of the northern and central plains were given two months in which to leave their homelands forever and report to assigned reservations. Snow lay drifted deep across the prairies that winter. The tribes probably couldn't have moved—even if they wanted to.

By February 1, the army was given the word to attack any tribes still unmoved. War was declared against the holdouts.

In rapid-fire series came United States Cavalry assaults on Sioux and Cheyenne, Kiowa and Comanche camps. The massing of troops centered around the Black Hills, where the gold strike brought thousands of prospectors swarming into the valleys with pickaxes and pans.

In spite of its written pledge to respect the Black Hills as the holy place of the Sioux, the United States government now tried to force the Indians out. Officials offered to buy the region for $6 million. A single mine, Homestake, would yield more than a hundred times that much in gold bullion. The Sioux refused to sell at any price.

At the time of the summer solstice, 1876, the Sioux gathered for their yearly Sun Dance. To the Plains Indians the Sun Dance ceremony was many things—a reunion to share a common heritage, a joyful celebration of life and its bounty, an occasion to plead for divine aid, a time for each person to renew his faith. In this troubled year, however, the Sioux were in mourning for their dead.

For four days the tribe gathered to fast and pray. They went through timeless rituals, dancing soberly and chanting a hymn to the sun. Their mood was despair. They sensed that this would be their last year in the shrine of their forefathers.

"Friends, it has been our misfortune to welcome the white man,"

Red Cloud told his people sadly. "We have been deceived. He brought with him some shining things that pleased our eyes. But to possess these things you must put away the wisdom of your fathers."

The Oglala chief denounced the efforts of the whites to break the spirits of the Indians by undermining their faith and destroying their religion. Most whites in fact saw the Indians as "heathen," "pagan," "godless," without any religion worthy of their respect.

Yet the Sioux were a devout people. Theirs was a religion of symbols, legends, and visions. Blue was the sky color, the symbol of the god Skan. Maka was the earth-goddess, the mother of all food and drink, symbolized in Sioux art by the color green.

Wi, the sun-god, was supreme. He was the source of all energy, all life. The sun was the bringer of health and cleanliness and growth. Wi was represented by the color red. And the Sun Dance was the Sioux worship of this benevolent deity.

As the Sun Dance of 1876 ended, federal troops, armed with rapid-fire weapons and field artillery unloosed a series of driving blows at the Sioux tribes. In the last days of June the Indians turned on their attackers briefly. A cavalry column, under Lt. Col. George Custer, struck at a Sioux village on the Little Bighorn. Custer and his men were wiped out in a short, fierce battle.

By late autumn, most of the Sioux had been rounded up and herded into the reservation. Red Cloud's Oglala were surrounded by the forces under Gen. George Crook. His situation hopeless, the chief was forced to surrender. His people were deprived of their horses and marched toward Camp Robinson.

Red Cloud was singled out for special humiliation. A large gathering was brought together under the guns of the cavalry. The army announced that the fiery Sioux leader was to be stripped of all his power. Red Cloud was no longer to be the chief of the Oglala, said General Crook.

Crushed by a superior force, the Sioux became one of the last Plains tribes to take up the hated routine of the reservation. This was an alien way of life. Wherever the Indians turned, they found themselves captives. They were hounded by government officials, who tried to force them to give up every shred of their Indian heritage.

"I am an Indian," Red Cloud sternly protested, "but you are trying to make a white man out of me!"

Once self-reliant, the tribesmen were now compelled to plead for government handouts. Leaders like Red Cloud were reduced to bargaining for beans and rice in order to keep their people from starving. In old age Red Cloud was a gaunt, sad-faced man, tormented by questions of how he might better have served his people and whether he had betrayed them in his dealings with white men.

In the raw March days of 1890 came strange news out of the Far West. An Indian savior had appeared on earth, preaching a message of hope. The young messiah, named Wovoka, reported a vision of the returning glory of Plains life, the reappearance of the vanished buffalo herds, the recovery of surrendered lands, the end of the invading white man.

A religion of revival spread like prairie wildfire. The new ritual was the Ghost Dance. Tribes long dispirited and lost in misery suddenly came to life. The Plains Indians saw the end of a terrible time. The Ghost Dance cast a spell of new faith over a wretched and doomed people.

Tribesmen on the reservations left the plough; gave up tending their half-starved cattle; deserted the white men's saloons, schoolhouses, and churches. They joined in the circling movements of the dance, chanting in unison, clothed in "ghost" shirts, which were believed to ward off the bullets of the white man.

Reports reaching Washington caused panic. Federal officials believed that the dancing Indians had gone mad, completely out of control. A government pledged to uphold freedom of worship could not tolerate this kind of religion! The Indian agents pleaded with the dancing tribes, and then threatened to cut off rations if they didn't stop. Military commanders were ordered into action.

Just before year's end, 1890, heavily armed cavalry surrounded a pitiful group of Indian families on the Sioux reservation at Wounded Knee Creek. A scuffle occurred, and some shots rang out. From the troops came a deafening salvo, cannonades from the Hotchkiss gun batteries, and the raking rapid volleys of repeating rifles. The drumfire continued until every Indian man, woman, child was dead. Many fell still wearing their ghost shirts.

The Indian religion of hope was no more. The Ghost Dance perished at Wounded Knee. With it went the last glimmering of the Indian faith that the old life on the Plains could ever be restored.

On a sweltering afternoon in July 1894, police near Casper, Wyoming, seized an old man whom they charged with trespassing, hunting out of season and without a license. This was Red Cloud, penniless and half-blind.

He might have told the judge that Indians had rights there older than any white man's deed or law, that he came from a long line of hunters to whom nature was a sacred trust, that it was not he nor his people who were spoiling the land or ravaging the wildlife.

Instead, Red Cloud remained silent. He paid his fine of sixty-six dollars by turning over his two horses. Then without a word, Red Cloud departed on foot, wandering off toward the sunset.

ROLL CALL OF FAME

PAWNEE, CHEYENNE, AND BLACKFOOT . . . Their hoofbeats still echo on the buffalo plains.

A hundred years ago they lived out their time of glory. Theirs was a vivid, spirited, flamboyant life while it lasted. Fleet horsemen, they spread across the prairies, a streak of color and splendor that has vanished forever.

Arapaho and Assiniboin, Crow and Comanche . . . The roll call of the Plains tribes goes on. In eagle feather warbonnets, painted faces, and fringed deerskin robes, they made a striking image against the drab grassland. Matchless bowmen and lancers, they rode to the hunt like the prairie wind.

Kiowa, Ponca, and Sioux . . . Their proud feats are still remembered. No one dishonors them because their dreams faded and their hopes died on the endless reaches of the prairie. They lost through no fault or weakness of their own. They simply met a might more powerful than themselves, a force that would not share the land or tolerate Indian ways.

On the dreary reservations where the Plains Indians now live, they still beat the rawhide drums and chant an old lament. They recall "a time when our hearts sang for joy." And people of goodwill seek some

92

measure of fair treatment for these descendants of conquered tribesmen.

In their time these tribes ran free across three million square miles of treeless flatlands. Once trackless and unmarred, the Great Plains later became the high road for America's westward expansion. The Indians of the grasslands stood briefly in the way of a nation driven by overpowering ambition. In time, towered cities arose over the cold ashes of tribal council fires. High overhead the jet trails now span prairies once crossed by immense buffalo herds. Stone faces of white men, carved into the cliffs of the Black Hills, stare out over sacred Indian lands.

Defeated, the Plains Indian of old has become the most famous of all Indians. Feared and hated by whites in his heyday, the mounted tribesman of the prairies can now be hallowed.

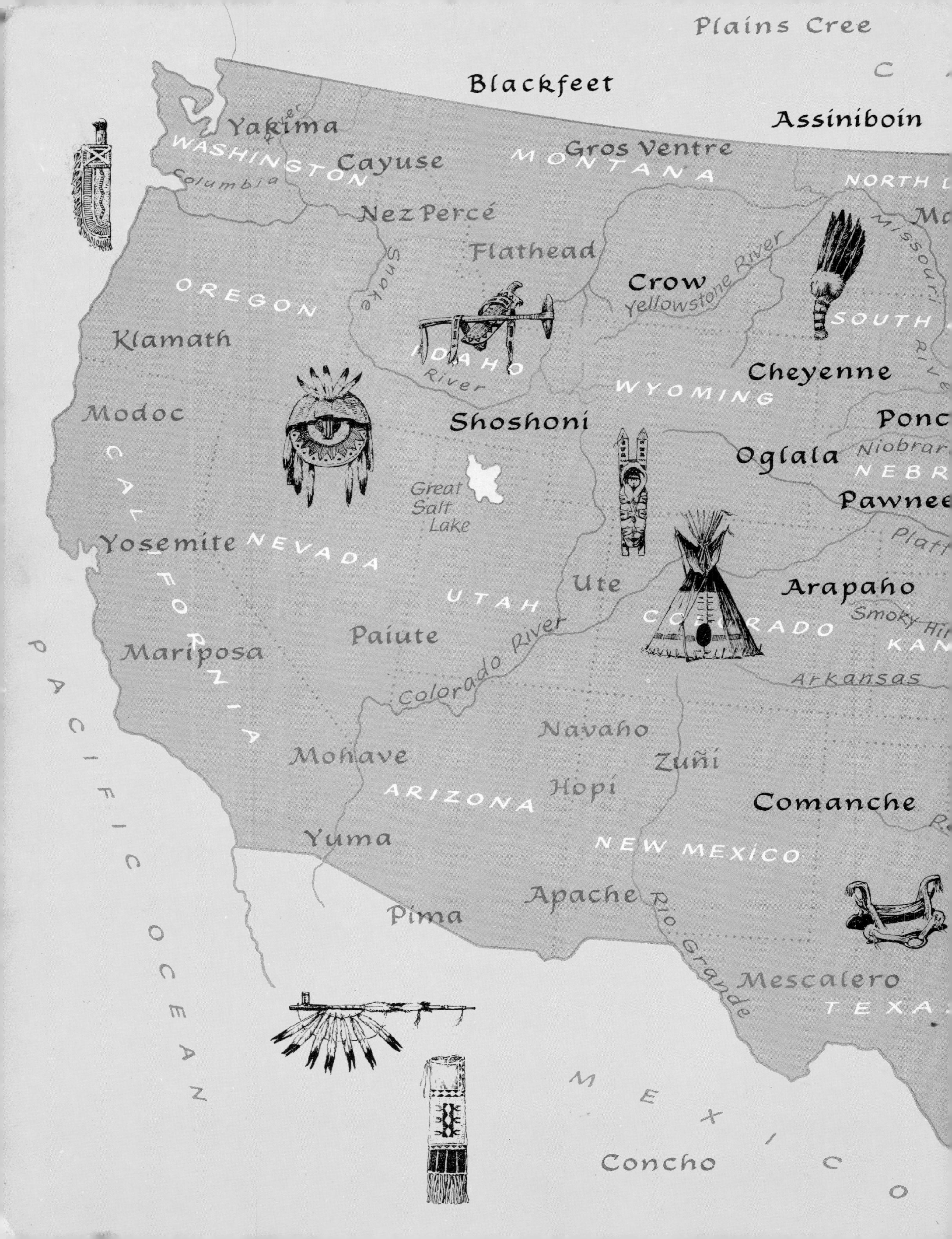

Plains Cree

Blackfeet

Assiniboin

Yakima

WASHINGTON

Columbia

Cayuse

Nez Percé

Flathead

Gros Ventre

MONTANA

NORTH D

Mo

Crow

Yellowstone River

Missouri River

SOUTH

OREGON

IDAHO

River

Snake

Cheyenne

WYOMING

Klamath

Shoshoni

Ponc

Oglala

Niobrar

NEBR

Modoc

Great
Salt
Lake

Pawnee

Platt

CALIFORNIA

Yosemite

NEVADA

Ute

Arapaho

Smoky Hil

UTAH

COLORADO

KAN

Paiute

Colorado River

Arkansas

Mariposa

PACIFIC OCEAN

Navaho

Zuñi

Mohave

ARIZONA

Hopi

Comanche

Yuma

NEW MEXICO

Pima

Apache

Rio Grande

Mescalero

TEXA

M E X I C O

Concho

Continued from inside of front cover

FAMOUS AMERICAN INDIANS of the Plains is their story from the coming of the horse to the last sad days of enforced farming on reservations. It covers every facet of their lives—from breaking horses to stealing them, from hunting buffalo to skinning them. Author Hirsch has compressed into these pages the whole fascinating world of these famous Indians. In addition, he explains the basic reasons behind the clashes between whites and Indians and the tragic misunderstandings which have not been reconciled to this date.

ABOUT THE AUTHOR ...

Author S. Carl Hirsch has written many books for children and young adults, several of which have won national awards. He feels that writing a book on the Plains Indians was a challenge for two reasons: first to convey the immense color and richness of their lives; second to cover the white-Indian conflict accurately and sympathetically but without sensationalism.

ABOUT THE ILLUSTRATOR ...

Lorence Bjorklund has illustrated many books including the other two books in Rand McNally's "Famous American" series, *Famous American Trails* and *Famous American Explorers*. He has collected Indian artifacts for years, and his knowledge of the American Indian is revealed by the accuracy and realism of his illustrations.

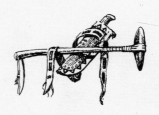

Date Due

SE 25 '75	UN 9 76	21	17
NO6 '75	SEP. 17 '76	1	24
NO14 '75	14	22	
NO28 '75	11	19	16
JAN 7 '76		17	
JAN 16 76	16	22	
11	16	15	
FEB 24 76	14	9	
MAR 22 '76	19	WH	
APR 20 '76	17	15	
MAY 28 76	7	18	

113435

ESEA TITLE II FY-74